The Tuskegee Airmen

by Philip Brooks

Content Adviser: Retired Major Joseph P. Gomer,
Tuskegee Airman, Duluth, Minnesota

Reading Adviser: Rosemary G. Palmer, Ph.D.,
Department of Literacy, College of Education,
Boise State University

This book is dedicated to Donald Hinz of Woodbury, Minnesota, who
died while flying a restored P-51C Mustang at an air show in May 2004.
Hinz was an experienced pilot and a member of the Commemorative
Air Force, which restores World War II planes. He coordinated the
Red Tail Project, which restored the rare World War II-era plane, the
Tuskegee Airmen, and honors the country's first black military pilots.

Compass Point Books ✦ **Minneapolis, Minnesota**

Compass Point Books
1710 Roe Crest Drive
North Mankato, MN 56003

On the cover: Pilots at the Tuskegee Army Airfield during World War II

Photographs ©: Library of Congress, cover, 11, 17, 31, 32, 36, 41; Hulton-Deutsch Collection/ Corbis, 4;
Hulton/Archive by Getty Images, 5, 7, 8, 9, 20; Bettmann/Corbis, 6, 13, 22, 35, 39; Stock Montage, Inc. 10;
Corbis, 12, 23, 38; U.S. Army Military History Institute, 14; Jack Delano/Corbis, 15; The photo courtesy of
the Chauncey E. Spencer Sr. Photo Family Collection, 18, 21; Carnegie Library of Pittsburgh, 19; National
Archives and Records Administration, 24, 25; Courtesy of Air Force Historical Research Agency, Maxwell Air
Force Base, Alabama, 26, 29, 30; Smithsonian National Air and Space Museum, 27; Gabriel Benzur/Time Life
Pictures/Getty Images, 33, 34; Paul Bowen/Redtail.org, 40.

Creative Director: Terri Foley
Managing Editor: Catherine Neitge
Photo Researcher: Marcie C. Spence
Designer/Page production: Bradfordesign, Inc./Jaime Martens
Cartographer: XNR Productions, Inc.

Library of Congress Cataloging-in-Publication Data
Brooks, Philip, 1963-
  Tuskegee airmen / by Philip Brooks.
      p. cm. — (We the people)
Includes bibliographical references and index.
ISBN 978-0-7565-0683-4 (hardcover)
ISBN 978-0-7565-1404-4 (paperback)
1. United States. Army Air Forces. Fighter Group, 332nd—History—Juvenile literature. 2. World War,
1939-1945—Participation, African American—Juvenile literature. 3. World War, 1939-1945—Aerial opera-
tions, American—Juvenile literature. 4. African Americans—Juvenile literature. 5. African American air
pilots—Juvenile literature. 6. Tuskegee Army Air Field (Ala.)—Juvenile literature. [1. United States. Army
Air Forces. Fighter Group, 332nd—History. 2. World War, 1939-1945—Participation, African American. 3.
World War, 1939-1945—Aerial operations, American. 4. African American air pilots. 5. Tuskegee Army Air
Field (Ala.)] I. Title. II. We the people (Series) (Compass Point Books)
D810.N4B76 2004
940.54'4973'08996073—dc22   2003024191

Quote on pages 20-21, as quoted by Chancey E. Spencer Sr.;
Quote on page 41, courtesy of Phyliss Gomer-Douglass, *Honor Thy Father: A Tuskegee Airman*

Visit Compass Point Books on the Internet at *www.capstonepub.com*
or e-mail your request to *custserv@compasspointbooks.com*

Printed in the United States of America in Eau Claire, Wisconsin.
060914   008299R

TABLE OF CONTENTS

NOTE: *In this book, words that are defined in the glossary are in* **bold** *the first time they appear in the text.*

DARK DAYS

During the early years of World War II (1939–1945), newspapers gave Americans plenty of bad news every day. The powerful armies of Nazi Germany, led by Adolf Hitler, were sweeping across Europe. Germany took over Czechoslovakia and Austria and would soon overrun

Belgium, Romania, and Greece. Hitler's forces terrorized and murdered Jews, Gypsies, and other ethnic groups he felt were **"impure."**

Soon German bombers attacked London and other British cities. Though politicians spoke out against Hitler, the United States stayed out

4

War news dominated newspapers around the world.

St. Paul's Cathedral stands above bombed, burning buildings in 1940 London.

of the fight. Everything changed on December 7, 1941. That day the Japanese navy attacked the United States Navy at Pearl Harbor in Hawaii. President Franklin Delano Roosevelt immediately declared war on Japan and Germany.

Roosevelt called upon every American to help win the war and protect freedom. African-Americans rose to the call. Thousands went to recruiting stations to sign up for the fight. The military, however, like much of the United States, was **segregated.** Black men who volunteered to fight and die for their country were not allowed to serve alongside whites. Special units were created for so-called "colored" soldiers.

5

Many American pilots were needed to fight in the skies above Europe. Pilots needed to be smart and brave. Flying fighter planes and bombers was complicated work that required a lot of training. Many qualified African-American men proudly volunteered to fly for the Army Air Corps. Their applications were rejected, however. Some military leaders believed that blacks were not physically or mentally fit to fly.

Many African-American men volunteered to serve their country.

African-Americans were disappointed in their country. Hitler believed Germans were part of a "master race." He hated groups of people he saw as being inferior to "pure" Germans. The United States fought Hitler's **racism,** yet it did nothing about its own. The U.S. military

Adolf Hitler

continued to enforce its own racist policies. Black leaders called for a "double war." First of all, they wanted to fight for the country they loved. At the same time, they would fight to prove black people were just as qualified to be pilots—or anything else—as white people.

7

FIGHTING TO FLY

In the years leading up to World War II, African-Americans were regularly denied equal treatment and opportunities. Segregation was widely accepted as a normal part of U.S. society. Separate and nearly always inferior facilities were created for African-Americans. In the South, **Jim Crow** laws and restrictions sent blacks to the back of public buses and denied them entry into "whites only" stores and restaurants. In some cases, these laws even took away their ability to vote in elections.

Worse, African-Americans were regularly kidnapped and murdered by white racists in order to create fear in the African-American

Blacks had to attend segregated movie theaters.

community and "keep them in their place." Such attacks were called lynchings. Though blacks living in the North were usually safe from physical attack, more subtle forms of racism made life difficult.

Many high-ranking military officials grew up in the South and believed blacks were inferior to whites. They placed limits on the numbers of blacks that could join the Army and Navy. Blacks who did join served mostly in kitchens or as janitors on Army bases.

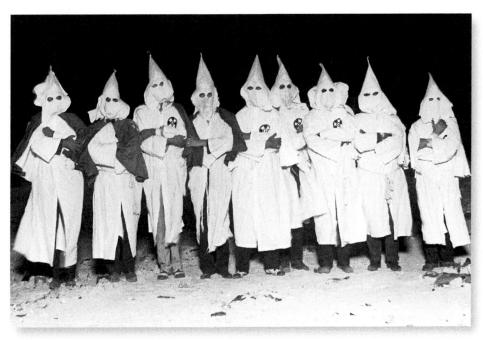

Members of the Ku Klux Klan threatened and attacked African-Americans.

9

After the Pearl Harbor attack, hundreds of African-American men appealed to President Roosevelt for relief from such **prejudice.** "I have applied at several recruiting stations at various times for enlistment in the Army Air Corps, only to have been refused … on the ground that I am a Negro," wrote a licensed pilot named Roderick Williams. "I appeal

Franklin Delano Roosevelt

to you for aid in securing the right to serve in the Army Air Corps without **discrimination** because of my color."

The National Association for the Advancement of Colored People (NAACP), African-American newspapers, and many white politicians and citizens argued that African-Americans deserved the same rights as white people. This included the right to become Army pilots.

In 1939, the U.S. Congress voted to allow the government to pay for flight training at schools run by nonmilitary instructors. The Civilian Pilot Training Program (CPTP) would allow people to learn the basics of flight without having to be part of the Army first. This was seen as a way that African-Americans might eventually be allowed into the Army Air Corps. After all, the Army desperately needed pilots to win the war. How could they ignore qualified black pilots?

An instructor works with a group of CPTP students in Maryland.

11

LEARNING TO BE PILOTS

By 1940, the NAACP had made equal opportunity in the military one of its most important goals. If African-Americans were allowed to fight for their country as equals, it would be harder for racists to say that blacks didn't deserve the same constitutional rights as whites.

The NAACP made African-American equality in the military a priority.

The campus of Tuskegee Institute in 1940

Thanks to white and black instructors in the CPTP, hundreds of African-Americans who were enrolled in black colleges and flight training schools learned the basics of flight.

Many African-Americans accepted into the program began training at the Tuskegee Institute, a black college in Tuskegee, Alabama, in December 1939. Because the school had no airfield, they had to travel to Montgomery, Alabama, about 40 miles (64 kilometers) away, to practice their actual flying. In addition to flying, they learned about using radios to communicate and maps to navigate. They also studied meteorology, which is the science of weather.

In 1939, there were only 125 licensed black pilots in the United States. A year later, 231 African-Americans had their pilot's licenses. Many believed that because they had studied hard to become pilots, they could now join the Army Air Corps. Major General E. S. Adams of the War Department had other ideas,

Major General E. S. Adams

however. He said flatly, "Applications from colored persons for flying cadet appointment or for enlistment in the air corps are not being accepted."

African-American newspapers such as the *Pittsburgh Courier* and *Chicago Defender* demanded not only that African-Americans be accepted as military pilots, but that the entire military be desegregated. A unified military could help unite the country, they said.

Even if they were sympathetic to such demands, most white military leaders argued that they could not change U.S. society. Their only job was to be ready for war. Other white officials believed black soldiers were inferior and would damage the military if allowed to enter in greater numbers. Those officers in favor of allowing greater participation by blacks were told to keep quiet or were moved out of positions

The Chicago Defender *was a leading black newspaper during the war.*

of authority. The military made statements supporting the rights of African-Americans but offered only vague promises of greater efforts to include them.

The NAACP and black newspapers stirred public opinion and kept pressure on the Army and politicians. In 1938, the *Pittsburgh Courier's* editor, Robert Vann, published the newspaper's "Ten Cardinal Points for Army and Navy Equality":

1. We deserve jobs in the services.
2. We pay for the jobs in the services.
3. Our fighting record should be rewarded.
4. We seek the test to prove our merit.
5. We need education just as the whites.
6. We seek a chance to shatter prejudice.
7. Our loyalty is an American tradition.
8. Americanism is the test of our fighting men.
9. We want to glorify America before the world.
10. We want to inspire future Black America.

The Pittsburgh Courier *demanded equality in the military.*

Vann was a powerful man with powerful friends. He worked heroically to force the military to admit black pilots. Vann called on President Roosevelt to speak out in support of African-Americans. Roosevelt, however, was afraid of angering whites in the South whose votes he needed for reelection, so he said little.

17

FREEDOM FLIERS

Dale White and Chauncey Spencer, two experienced African-American pilots, took off from Chicago on May 9, 1939. Their plan was to fly 3,000 miles (4,800 kilometers), with stops in various cities, to promote the skill and daring of black pilots. When funding for the trip fell through, the two men refused to give up. They managed to collect enough cash to rent an old **biplane** that had no lights, brakes, or advanced flying instruments.

The plane, which they named *Old Faithful,* had engine trouble over Ohio.

Chauncey Spencer

18

They managed a bumpy landing in a farmer's field. After installation of a new crankshaft, the pair took off and headed for Morgantown, West Virginia. The airport's white crew chief refused to allow them to park their plane in a hangar. He urged them to quickly refuel and head for Pittsburgh.

Robert Vann

The pair filled their tank, took off, then managed to follow a much larger commercial plane into the Allegheny County Airport. They were promptly grounded in Pittsburgh for violating regulations meant to keep small and large planes from colliding. Only Robert Vann and his *Pittsburgh Courier* kept the two men flying. Vann used his legal skill and political friends to get the charges dropped.

White and Spencer eventually continued on to Washington, D.C., where they met Senator Harry S. Truman of Missouri. Impressed with their journey, Truman asked them whether they had applied for the Army Air Corps. The two aviators told him there was no point since African-American pilots were always rejected. Truman seemed surprised, and they asked for the senator's help in righting this wrong.

Truman asked to see *Old Faithful.* After seeing the condition of the plane, the future president of the United States said, "If you had the guts to fly this thing to Washington,

Harry Truman

20

Enoch P. Waters Jr., editor of the Chicago Defender *(center) greets Dale White (left) and Chauncey Spencer on their return to Chicago in May 1939.*

I've got the guts enough to see that you get what you are asking." When the two men returned to Chicago, they found a hero's welcome awaiting them.

A PARTIAL VICTORY

In the winter of 1940, an African-American man named Yancey Williams applied for entry into the Air Corps and was denied. Williams was a licensed pilot and a Howard University student. He had passed an Army physical and was clearly qualified to become a cadet. Williams decided to go to court to force the United States government to let him join.

The day after Williams filed his lawsuit, the Army Air Corps agreed to train a **squadron** of African-American pilots. Williams dropped his suit. He would be one of the first to earn the silver wings of the Air Corps.

The new squadron was dedicated at Tuskegee Institute in 1941.

The new 99th Pursuit Squadron would include 33 black pilots and 278 mechanics and ground crew members. The Army made it clear that no African-American fliers would be allowed to serve alongside whites.

General George C. Marshall

Many blacks were unhappy with what the Air Corps called "an experiment." They wanted to serve as equal members of the military. General George C. Marshall, the Army Chief of Staff, explained: "Segregation is an established American custom. … Experiments within the Army in the evolution of social problems are fraught with danger to efficiency, discipline, and morale." Black leaders and many whites rejected this argument. If black and white soldiers got to know one another, they argued, they would get along just fine.

A group of recruits reports to Tuskegee Institute in 1941.

Meanwhile, hundreds of African-American men volunteered for the new squadron. Many of these volunteers were college-educated and highly qualified. Thirty-five who scored highest on the Army's intelligence tests were chosen to report to Tuskegee Institute for more training. The Army was surprised that so many applicants did so well on the tests. Those who completed the training successfully would become pilots.

In addition to the pilots, several hundred other volunteers were accepted for training at Chanute Field in Illinois. These men became airplane mechanics, **armament** specialists, radio repairmen, parachute riggers, control tower operators, policemen, and administrative personnel. The Tuskegee Airmen spoke proudly of the skill and dedication of these less-famous members of the African-American squadrons.

The mechanics of the 99th Pursuit Squadron were important to the unit's success.

TUSKEGEE INSTITUTE

Since black pilots were not allowed to share runways with whites, a new training facility had to be constructed. The Army chose Tuskegee Institute as the site for a new air base.

Tuskegee Institute, a distinguished black college founded by Booker T. Washington in 1881, was already the site of the Civilian Pilot Training Program. The eastern Alabama area had good weather and low air traffic.

The college enjoyed one huge advantage over any other location. A man named Charles Alfred Anderson was in charge of Tuskegee's basic flight training. Known as "Chief," Anderson taught hundreds of African-American students how

Charles Anderson (second from right) taught hundreds of students how to fly.

26

to fly and became a hero to many.

One bright spring day in 1941, Eleanor Roosevelt, the wife of President Franklin D. Roosevelt, visited Tuskegee Institute. She privately wondered whether African-Americans could become

Charles Anderson took Eleanor Roosevelt for a spin.

good pilots—until Anderson took her on a flight above the green hills of Alabama. Roosevelt was so impressed with Anderson's flying skill and his personal charm that she became a strong supporter of African-American aviation.

Construction on what would be called Tuskegee Army Airfield began in 1941. McKissack and McKissack, a construction company owned and operated by African-Americans, was hired to build the facility. Crews cleared

27

land and built a tent city to serve as temporary quarters for the new recruits.

Much was expected of the young cadets. Fewer than half would successfully complete the training and become officers and pilots in the 99th Pursuit Squadron.

Tuskegee is in eastern Alabama.

Louis Purnell described a typical day of training: "We'd all go down to the flying line … and stand before our instructors. The instructors would come out and tell you, 'Aviator

Some Tuskegee Airmen signed this photo.

Cadet Louis Purnell, we're going up to 10,000 feet, and we'll perform loops and slow rolls, etc.' You'd wait your turn, then you'd go up. Instructors would say very little during instruction, but they were strict. When you came down there was no exchange of words. He had a little slip and so many errors would amount to a pink slip and so many pink slips and you're out." If a cadet got three pink slips, he was dropped from the flight program.

Conditions at the new airbase were difficult. Water had to be trucked in to the tent city, and meals were prepared in simple field kitchens. Mud was often ankle deep.

The tent city at Tuskegee

Some white residents of Tuskegee also made things difficult for the cadets. They resented having a segregated African-American base in their town. Blacks who left the base to shop or dine out often suffered **indignities** despite their uniforms. They knew they had to endure such painful insults without lashing out. If they showed their anger, **bigots** in the military might argue the "experiment" was a failure.

The sheriff in the town of Tuskegee, Pat Evans, was a particularly disgusting character. He enjoyed bothering uniformed African-American servicemen whenever they entered town. He addressed black officers as "boy" and gave them tickets for jaywalking or speeding. In one incident, he even disarmed a black military policeman.

READY AND WAITING

At the end of five weeks of flight training, five cadets graduated to the final training phase: Lemuel Custis, Charles DeBow, Mac Ross, George S. Roberts, and Benjamin O. Davis Jr. On March 7, 1942, the first class of pilots earned their wings. In the summer, Davis was promoted from captain to lieutenant colonel and named commander of the 99th Fighter Squadron.

The first class of pilots to earn their wings: (from left) George S. Roberts, Benjamin O. Davis Jr., Charles DeBow, instructor R.M. Long, Mac Ross, and Lemuel Custis.

31

Benjamin O. Davis Jr. climbed into the cockpit of an advanced trainer plane.

Davis was nearly 30 years old, several years older than any of the other men. His father, Brigadier General Benjamin Davis Sr., was the highest-ranking African-American in the Army. Davis Jr. had graduated from West Point Academy, the Army's strict and highly regarded college. During his four years, he was the only African-American cadet. He received the "silent treatment" from fellow cadets because he was black. Despite such constant pressure, Davis finished among the top 40 students of his class.

The 99th had a respected commander and was soon at full strength. Tuskegee Airfield became home to more than 3,000 men. While the Army regularly announced that qualified white volunteers were needed to train immediately as pilots, hundreds of fully qualified black men waited on a list for a chance to become cadets.

As the war raged across Europe and into northern Africa, the pilots and crew of the 99th stood ready in

An Army officer taught members of the 99th as they awaited their call for duty.

Alabama. They practiced their flying every day, anxiously waiting for orders that would send them into action. Months passed. New black pilots formed the 100th, 301st, and 302nd Fighter Squadrons. Still, by the end of 1942, none of the African-American

Colonel Benjamin O. Davis Jr. was greeted by fellow pilots.

pilots had received orders sending them into combat. Many of the men became frustrated and disappointed.

At a flying exhibition held at Tuskegee, Colonel Davis told a crowd that black pilots at Tuskegee were performing just as well as white pilots. The *Chicago Defender* quoted him as saying, "My greatest desire is to lead this squadron to victory against the enemy."

34

During this time, the white man who commanded Tuskegee Air Base, Colonel Frederick Von Kimble, did all he could to make life miserable for the African-American officers and enlisted men. He enforced "colored" and "whites only" toilets on the base and other humiliating Jim Crow rules. When black officers protested, they were told they had better "accept the rules and like them."

The black pilots continued to train despite their frustrations.

FINALLY GETTING THEIR CHANCE

The 99th waited through the winter of 1942 for orders to join the fighting. Finally, on April 15, 1943, the men of the 99th boarded a ship bound for Morocco in North Africa. They shared the boat with 3,400 white troops. Colonel Benjamin Davis Jr. was put in charge of all the soldiers while on the ship.

The Tuskegee Airmen finally got their orders in April 1943.

Once the ship docked, the 99th went to their training base near the town of Fez. The men liked Morocco. "The town of Fez was found to be one of the most delightful spots any of us had ever visited," wrote Davis Jr.

He also mentioned a positive interaction with a group of white pilots: "Four P-39 pilots whom we had met on the boat on the way over ... stopped by to pay us a visit. I mention this simply to indicate that a considerable bond existed among those who fly regardless of color or race." This would be true throughout the war. The men who did the actual flying and fighting generally respected the men of the 99th as pilots and fellow soldiers.

After further waiting and more training, the 99th saw its first action against enemy planes. While on a patrol over Pantelleria, an island off the coast of Italy, six P-40 fighter planes piloted by members of the 99th spotted 12 German fighter planes. The men of the 99th circled and soared trying to gain a favorable position. The German machine guns blazed. One of the P-40s was hit but not damaged badly.

P-40 fighter planes

Soon, more German fighters attacked, and the men of the 99th fought back. "One enemy aircraft was last seen at 1,800 feet excessively smoking," says the official mission report from that day.

"It was the first time any of them had ever shot at the enemy," reported Davis Jr. "They gave a good account of themselves considering the odds against them, and, most important, they all came back safely."

In June 1944, the 99th Fighter Squadron joined the 332nd Fighter Group, which consisted of three squadrons of Tuskegee Airmen—the 100th, the 301st, and the 302nd. The pilots were assigned to escort groups of bombers as they went on missions to destroy targets in Italy. The huge bombers were slow moving, and the smaller, faster fighter planes protected them against enemy attack. In more than

200 missions over most of central and southern Europe, the Tuskegee Airmen never lost a bomber to an attack by an enemy plane—a remarkable record.

When the Tuskegee Airmen were provided with P-47 fighter planes, and later, P-51 Mustangs, they painted the tails bright red so that bombers they were escorting, as well as enemy pilots, would know who they were. German pilots feared and respected the pilots of the 332nd. They called them *Schwartze Vogelmenschen* or "Black Birdmen."

Tuskegee Airmen in Italy shared stories after a raid in 1944.

American bomber crews who knew of their reputation for never losing a plane nicknamed them "Red Tail Angels."

P-51C Mustang with its signature red tail

The Tuskegee Airmen flew more than 15,000 missions in North Africa, Italy, and Germany. They destroyed or damaged 409 enemy planes and escorted more than 200 bomber missions that helped to finally defeat Germany and free Europe from Hitler's grip in June 1945. Seventy-eight members of the 332nd died during the war, and 32 were taken prisoner. They earned 150 Distinguished Flying Crosses, eight Purple Hearts, and countless other honors and awards for bravery and service.

Their sacrifices in combat reveal only a part of the service these men gave to the United States. The Tuskegee Airmen showed a rare form of courage as they battled racist attitudes within the military.

40

"We were fighting two battles," said retired Major Joseph P. Gomer. "I flew for my parents, for my race, for our battle for first-class citizenship and for my country. We were fighting for the 14 million black Americans back home. We were there to break down barriers, open a few doors, and do a job."

Proud and intelligent men, the Tuskegee Airmen suffered insults and unfair treatment without lashing out or giving up. Their quiet strength earned the respect of many of those who had opposed letting them fly. Like Martin Luther King Jr., Rosa Parks, and Jackie Robinson, their dignity in the face of cruelty and ignorance inspired a change in the way Americans viewed their country.

A Tuskegee Airman at Ramitelli, Italy, in March 1945

GLOSSARY

armament—weapons, ammunition, and supplies used to fight a war

bigots—people who treat people of another race with hatred

biplane—a small aircraft with two sets of wings fixed at different levels

discrimination—treating people unfairly because of their race, religion, sex, or age

impure—not pure; racists use the term to indicate a person is of mixed race or ethnic origin

indignities—acts that cause offense and insult

Jim Crow—discrimination against blacks by rules and laws

prejudice—hatred or unfair treatment of a group of people who belong to a certain race or religion

racism—the belief that one race is better than others

segregated—when people of different races are kept apart

squadron—a unit of the military

DID YOU KNOW?

- In 1921, Bessie Coleman became the first African-American woman to be granted a pilot's license. She performed stunts at air shows across the country and became known as "Brave Bessie."

- Tuskegee's 477th Bombardment Group never saw action in Europe, but its members fought discrimination at home. In April 1945, 60 officers stationed at Freeman Field in Indiana were arrested when they tried to enter a segregated officers' club. More than 100 black officers were later arrested. Following these peaceful protests, the white officer in charge, who had enforced a strict segregation policy, was replaced. Colonel Benjamin O. Davis Jr. then became the first African-American to command an Air Force base in the United States.

- Donald Hinz was a Minnesota pilot who coordinated a nine-year restoration of a rare P-51C Mustang, *Tuskegee Airmen.* He died when the historic plane he was flying crashed at an air show in May 2004.

- In 1948, President Harry S. Truman enacted an executive order that began desegregation of the armed forces of the United States.

- The National Park Service is interviewing the surviving Tuskegee Airmen as part of an oral history project to save the stories of America's first black military pilots. The project will be part of a planned museum at the Tuskegee Airmen National Historic Site.

IMPORTANT DATES

Timeline

1939	After listening to the appeals of black pilots unable to enter the military, Senator Harry S. Truman sponsors a bill to create the Civilian Pilot Training Program.
1941	The United States enters World War II.
1942	First class of black pilots trained at Tuskegee Institute earn their wings from the Army Air Corps.
1944	Black fighter squadrons see combat in Europe.
1945	Germany and Japan surrender, ending World War II.
1948	President Harry S. Truman enacts an executive order to begin desegregation of the armed forces of the United States.
1998	Benjamin O. Davis Jr. earns the rank of four-star general; Congress creates the Tuskegee Airmen National Historic Site at Moton Field in Tuskegee, Alabama.

IMPORTANT PEOPLE

BENJAMIN O. DAVIS JR. (1912–2002)

Commander of the 332nd Fighter Group who went on to become the first black general in the U.S. Air Force

HARRY S. TRUMAN (1884–1972)

U.S. senator who sponsored a bill to create the Civilian Pilot Training Program and U.S. president who desegregated the armed forces

BOOKER T. WASHINGTON (1856–1915)

African-American educator and founder of the Tuskegee Institute in Alabama

ROBERT L. VANN (1879–1940)

African-American editor of the Pittsburgh Courier *who campaigned to admit black pilots into the Army*

WANT TO KNOW MORE?

More Books to Read

George, Linda, and Charles George. *The Tuskegee Airmen.* Danbury, Conn.:
   Children's Press, 2001.

Harris, Jacqueline. *The Tuskegee Airmen: Black Heroes of World War II.*
   Parsipanny, N.J.: Dillon Press, 1996.

McKissack, Patricia, and Frederick McKissack. *Red-Tail Angels: The
   Story of the Tuskegee Airmen of World War II.* New York: Walker
   and Company, 1995.

On the Web

For more information on this topic, use FactHound.

1. Go to *www.facthound.com*

2. Type in this book ID: 0756506832

3. Click on the *Fetch It* button.

FactHound will find the best Web sites for you.

On the Road

Tuskegee Institute National Historic Site

1212 W. Montgomery Road

Tuskegee Institute, AL 36088

334/727-3200

To learn more about Booker T. Washington's Tuskegee Institute,

located on the Tuskegee University campus

Tuskegee Airmen National Historic Site

1616 Chappie James Ave.

Tuskegee, AL 36083

334/724-0922

To learn more about the 1942–1946 "Tuskegee Experience"

National Air and Space Museum

Independence Avenue at Fourth Street Southwest

Washington, DC 20560

202/357-2700

To see the largest collection of air and spacecraft in the world

INDEX

About the Author

Philip Brooks lives in Gambier, Ohio, with his wife, Balinda, along with five tortoises and two parakeets. He writes nonfiction books for young readers as well as fiction for adults. He loves to read, cook, and play basketball.